Things to Think On

Every Day Bible Devotions and Meditations Volume 3

Dr. Michael L. Williams
Pamela Rose Williams

Christianity Every Day

Things to Think On: Every Day Bible Devotions and Meditations Volume 3

Dr. Michael L. Williams and Pamela Rose Williams

Copyright © 2024 by Christianity Every Day

Published by Christianity Every Day, United States of America

www.christianityeveryday.com

ISBN: 978-0-9996173-9-7

All rights reserved. No part of this publication may be reproduced, stored in a retrieval system, or transmitted in any form or by any means: electronic, mechanical, photocopy, recording, or otherwise without prior permission of the author, unless permitted under Sections 107 or 108 of the 1976 United States Copyright Act.

Scripture quotations are from the Holy Bible, King James Version. Printed in the United States of America.

A Note From The Authors

Here is another installment of 31 daily devotions that you can use as you begin your day with "Things to Think On".

What is great about these little books is that even if there are less than 31 days in the month, no worries! Double or triple up at the end of the month. You simply cannot get too much of God's Word in your day and in your heart!

Remember to tell someone about these little books. They are great as gifts, and we have found them especially helpful for someone who is ill and housebound.

God's peace be with you.

Michael & Pamela Rose

BE STRONG

Key Bible Passage: Ephesians 6:10 Finally, my brethren, be strong in the Lord, and in the power of his might.

When you read this verse from Paul's letter to the Ephesians, it sounds like he is wrapping it up, closing the letter. But the truth of the matter is that he is just getting started. His conclusion does not really begin until verse 19.

So then, if he is not presenting a conclusion, what is he saying? Be strong in the Lord! I believe Paul is encouraging us to count on the Lord when we are faced with battles that seem to be impossible to overcome. In fact, when we read on, Paul even gives us some great advice on "how" we can "be strong in the Lord". He speaks of the armour that is needed to stand against spiritual darkness.

You see, it is true that we are saved from certain death by faith in what Jesus did for us on the cross at Calvary. Even so, in this present world our flesh still battles against "spiritual wickedness in high places" (Ephesians 6:12). Paul encourages us to stand strong with the breastplate of righteousness. He incites us to remember that we should also be prepared with the gospel of peace, and that faith is our shield which protects us from all of Satan's fiery darts. The word picture continues as he speaks of the helmet of salvation and the sword of the Spirit.

And this is not to forget that prayer is also an essential part of our armour as we stand strong in the Lord (Ephesians 6:18-20). Perhaps my favorite part of Ephesians 6 comes when Paul asks the church to pray for him -- that when he opens his mouth that he might speak boldly the mystery of the gospel. Even this man, the one whom was inspired by the Holy Spirit to write thirteen (or maybe fourteen if we count Hebrews) books of the Bible, knows how important prayer is. He knows that his strength was in the Lord and that he needed the saints to pray so that he would remain strong to make known the gospel of Jesus Christ.

Are you using all of the tools and weapons that God has given to the believer to keep Satan at bay? Do you know that you have what it takes to "Be Strong"? How is your prayer life? Do you find yourself praying for others more than praying for yourself? Do you remember to give thanks daily for all that Jesus has done for you?

When we are in Christ, we have everything we need to "Be Strong" in the Lord. Sometimes we just need to remember that we cannot be strong without Him. How wonderful is it that we have a Mighty Savior? Selah

WALKING IN THE WAY

Key Bible Passage: Psalms 119:1 Blessed are the undefiled in the way, who walk in the law of the LORD.

The book of Psalms contains 150 songs, poems, and praises written by David and several others. Of particular note is the fact that they also reflect events, and times, and truths that can be found in Scripture. However, they are not just a collection of these and other quaint sayings, but we also find that they play an important role in the mental well-being of humanity.

In 1 Samuel 16:14-23 we find an early application of the Psalms to the life of King Saul. At the beginning of the chapter God told the Prophet Samuel to fill his horn with oil and go to Bethlehem to anoint a new king over Israel. God had rejected Saul from continuing to be the King of Israel because he had turned his back from following God and had not followed what God had told him to do (1 Samuel 15:10-11). Because of this, Samuel was bitterly grieving God's decision to reject Saul.

Samuel left as God had commanded and after arriving at Bethlehem, he encountered David's father. After some examination of his sons, God told Samuel that David was the one He had selected because of what was in David's heart. Samuel anointed David as God had commanded

In the very next verse after this happened, we find that the Spirit of the LORD departed from Saul and an evil spirit from the LORD troubled him (1 Samuel 16:14). Saul's servants suggested that they have someone come and play music for Saul so that he might feel better. Saul agreed and one of the servants proposed that they bring David to play for him – "…a son of Jesse the Bethlehemite, that is cunning in playing, and a mighty valiant man, and a man of war, and prudent in matters, and a comely person, and the LORD is with him." Saul agreed to this and ordered that David be brought there.

Word was sent to David's father and David was sent. Before long, Saul came to love and trust David. He sent word again to David's father saying that David had found favor in his sight and asked that David remain there to play music for Saul.

It is then that we learn that when the evil spirit from God was upon Saul that David took a harp and played music for Saul. Saul was refreshed and was well, and the evil spirit departed from Saul.

Many of us are comforted by music. However, the music that David played was accompanied by lyrics that later came to be known as the Psalms. We find that it was not the music that made the evil spirit depart, it was the word of God that were the lyrics to the songs.

Psalms 119 tells of God's truth as found in his Word and how His directions to us produce results. His Word is quick, powerful, and sharper than any two-edged sword and is able to divide our soul and spirit from our joints and marrow. Simply stated the Psalms teach us that God's Word has the power of God to effect change in us. However, change depends on obedience to follow the directions that God gives us.

Finally, Psalms 119:1 tells us that God will bless those whom are undefiled or cleansed of our sins in salvation and walk in His nurture and admonition. May God bless us as we rely on Him to empower us to do the same.

BLESSED TO LOVE AND SERVE

Key Bible Passage: Exodus 23:25 And ye shall serve the Lord your God, and he shall bless thy bread, and thy water; and I will take sickness away from the midst of thee.

The book of Exodus mainly concentrates on the deliverance of the Israelites out of the bondage in Egypt. It is in this book that the Ten Commandments are first mentioned (chapter 20). And then in chapters 21-24 Moses writes down many other laws that God gave.

During the "Exodus" times in the Bible, the Hebrew people trusted Moses to lead them into the Promised Land. They learned of the one true God from Moses and trusted Him to provide for their every need -- even amidst the 40 days and 40 nights that they spent wandering in the wilderness after escaping Egypt. In God's Law He reminded the people that He was the Only God that they should serve and as they served Him, He would continue to bless them with good food and water. He even went so far as to protect them from sickness. As you read further on into the

Old Testament, such as in the Book of Joshua and Judges you see that when the people served only Almighty God and Father, He was faithful to deliver on His promises. And when they left Him to serve other gods, they suffered great hardship, sickness and even death.

Things are not so different today. As Solomon wrote "...there is no new thing under the sun" (Ecclesiastes 1:9). We still have only One True God and there are those who choose to follow Him and those who choose to follow after other gods. Today, all of those hundreds of laws in the Old Testament have been contained in these two: (1) Love the Lord your God with all your heart soul and mind and (2) Love your neighbor as yourself (Matthew 22:34-40).

Think about it, when we go against either of these two "Great Commandments" we lose out on blessings. The first, "Love the Lord your God" - We love God by: remembering that He is the Only God, remembering that He is most important above all other idols, remembering that His name is holy and should never be taken in vain, and by remembering that we all need a day of rest, just as He did after He created the world. And the second, "Love your neighbor" - We love our neighbor by: showing honor to our parents, not killing each other, not committing adultery, working with our own hands so we do not have to steal from one another, speaking the truth in love rather than lying, and by being content with what we have rather than coveting the things of others.

Truth be told, not everyone loves God or his neighbor. Sometimes we even see that these Godless haters appear to be blessed with many earthly things. But that is exactly it - they are "earthly" and temporary. We are blessed to love and serve for a higher calling - that unspeakable eternal gift found only in Jesus Christ.

BLESSED ASSURANCE OF GRACE

Key Bible Passage: Psalms 119:2-3 Blessed are they that keep his testimonies, and that seek him with the whole heart. They also do no iniquity: they walk in his ways.

If you ask most people what they think of when they hear the word testimony, they will respond in context with a description of someone giving information as a witness in a court case. Likewise, we see from our devotional verses that they are given in the context of the previous verse (one), which refers to the Lord. Therefore, we can understand this verse to say that Blessed are they that keep his [The Lord's] testimonies.

God shows His love by blessing, which is a visual demonstration to His creation of His grace. More specifically, He demonstrates His grace through blessing those whom keep His testimonies. In the parable of the Sower, Jesus described four situations where the seed was sown, and a result was seen. He told how the first seed sown fell by the wayside and the birds came and ate it. The second seed was sown on stony ground and sprung up, but it had no roots and the heat of the day withered and killed it. The third seed fell amongst the thorns and the thorns grew up and choked it, so it yielded no fruit. Finally, the fourth seed was sown on good rich soil, and it grew to produce a multitude of fruit. Jesus concluded this parable by saying that the seed was the Word of God that is sown in our hearts.

God's Word is a testimony to us. The birth, life, and death of Jesus is a living testimony of God to us. The spoken Word by the prophets and apostles is a spoken testimony of God to us. Finally, the written Word is the record of their testimony as the written testimony of God to us.

When we seek after the Lord's testimonies, we are planting His Word into our hearts. God also tells us that our heart is deceitful above all things and desperately wicked to the point of questioning who can know it (Jeremiah 17:9). However, God does know our hearts and like the seeds sown, His testimonies result in blessings in whose heart the seed remains.

In verse two, God also issues a directive that He will bless those that keep His testimonies and seek him with their whole heart. This sets up a pattern of testimonies of directives from God in Psalms that are followed by results that He will bring to pass by His blessed grace.

The result of us receiving God's blessing by His grace is that legally, justice is served in His courtroom. It is not by works of righteousness which we have done, but according to His mercy He saved us and made us clean – without iniquity or its legal implication in His sight.

Furthermore, Because of God's grace, He has empowered us to walk in His ways, not out of fear of suffering His wrath. But, motivated by His love to walk in His ways because He has delivered us from the wrath to come! We then seek to please Him because we love Him. We love Him because He first demonstrated His love for us by giving us His unspeakable gift of salvation.

Let us draw close to God, devoting time to sowing and keeping His testimonies in our heart. Let us respond in whole-hearted love by walking in His ways and demonstrating His love to others throughout our day.

Make Up Your Mind

Key Bible Passage: James 1:6 But let him ask in faith, nothing wavering. For he that wavereth is like a wave of the sea driven with the wind and tossed.

Do you know anyone like that? Someone who says one thing and does another. Oh! Maybe it is you that does that. Come on, we have all had those times when we just can't make up our mind as to what we are going to do. Or maybe we try it several different ways, just in case. And then we crash and burn.

This verse in James 1 is preceded by a verse that we often miss: *"If any of you lack wisdom, let him ask of God, that giveth to all men liberally, and upbraideth not; and it shall be given him"* (James 1:5).

So, why is it so difficult for us to make up our mind? The Bible clearly says that if we lack wisdom we should ask for God's help. And it even goes on to remind us that God "upbraideth not". That is an Old English way of saying God will not scold or criticize us when we ask of Him.

I would venture to say that we don't ask for help because in our human pride, we think we already have all the answers – all the wisdom. So, we try to work it out our own way. In fact, back in Old Testament times when every man did what he thought was right in his own eyes things just went downhill from there (Read also, Judges chapter 21). It was not that they chose to do wrong, they simply chose to do what "they" thought was right. They did not follow the Lord. They did not ask for wisdom. In fact, didn't this all start way back in the Garden when Adam and Eve ate from the forbidden tree – they wanted to decide for themselves what was good and what was evil.

God gave us a brain and even reasoning ability so that we could make decisions. But more importantly, He gave us His very Word so that we could make up our mind to do what pleases Him.

When we are faced with an important decision, and we cannot decide what to do we need to ask the Lord for His wisdom. He gives it freely and without strings. When we know God's Word we will not be "tossed to and fro" in the storms of life. We will be able to make up our mind, God's way. Trust Him!

ASKING FOR DIRECTIONS

Key Bible Passage: Psalms 119:4-5 Thou hast commanded us to keep thy precepts diligently. O that my ways were directed to keep thy statutes!

Every one of us knows someone that is notorious for not stopping to ask for directions. They will often drive around for hours looking for a destination. Despite the time they take in their fruitless search, they will just not stop to ask anyone for directions on how to get where they want to go.

To make matters worse, some that do this even have GPS systems in their vehicle. Yet, even with it taking only a minute to enter the destination or ask their device for directions they will instead drive off thinking they already know how to get there.

God tells us to keep His precepts diligently. A precept is a rule or general way of thinking to keep in mind before doing something. For example, a precept to keep in mind when handling eggs is that they easily break. Therefore, we should keep this in mind when we pick up or handle the eggs. If we forget this precept, then the chances of us breaking an egg are great.

At the same time, God says to keep them diligently. Doing this assures that we are consistent to pay close attention and use caution in keeping God's precepts when we do something. The result is that we keep God's way of doing things in our mind and they are not forgotten, which gives us direction in how we go.

If we think about it, why does God direct us to do this? It is not to make our life miserable. But, instead, He wants to provide a reliable perspective in how we think and live our lives. More specifically, He wants our sense of direction to be aimed toward His perfect sense of direction.

Jesus taught that the Old Testament laws include not just our actions, but our thoughts that are related to our actions. When we were commanded not to steal, the New Testament told us instead to work with our hands so that we can give to those whom have need. When we were commanded not to lie, the Old Testament instead told us to speak the truth in love. One-by-one as we look at Old Testament commands, we see a New Testament directive to do things that are the opposite of what we were commanded not to do.

In matters of stealing, how can we steal if we are focused on working to provide for the needs of others? In matters of lying, how can we lie if we are focused on telling the truth? We see then that God wants us to follow His precepts to get in the right direction instead of ignoring His precepts and going in the wrong direction.

When we put it all together, God wants us to study His precepts or ways so that they become a second or "new" nature that we use as a basis to do things. To learn His precepts, we must read and meditate on His Word and hide it deep in our heart. This will provide new directions that lead us to do things how He would want them done.

Let us consider how much time we spend learning His precepts. Let us diligently ask Him for directions instead of driving off in the ways we think we should go. In doing so, we can demonstrate how asking Him for the right directions can change lives headed in the wrong direction.

My Buckler

Key Bible Passage: Psalms 18:1-2 I will love thee, O Lord, my strength. The Lord is my rock, and my fortress, and my deliverer; my God, my strength, in whom I will trust; my buckler, and the horn of my salvation, and my high tower.

Sometimes in my devotions I come across a great Old English word. Today I saw the word "buckler" surrounded by all of these other words that are used by the Psalmist to describe the Lord.

We have heard the Lord described as "my strength" and "my rock" and even "my fortress", but this word "buckler"…this was a new one for me. So, I had to look it up! I often say that when you are studying the Bible sometimes you need some other helps nearby. It is good to have a concordance of some type as well as a Bible dictionary. But in this case, I needed a good Old English dictionary. So, I went to the Webster's 1828 Dictionary and found this definition:

"BUCK'LER, noun A kind of shield, or piece of defensive armor, anciently used in

war. It was composed of wood, or wickers woven together, covered with skin or leather, fortified with plates of brass or other metal, and worn on the left arm. On the middle was an umbo, boss or prominence, very useful in causing stones and darts to glance off. The buckler often was four feet long, and covered the whole body."

Well, that explained it! As so very often times the Psalmist is discussing battles and war, and sometimes even trying to escape his real enemy. I love how he used a great picture of battle armour to illustrate how very much we are under the Lord's protection. This "buckler" was an essential piece of the body armour used by ancient warriors. It was actually THE shield that protected the entire body … especially the heart.

That "buckler" warded off stones and darts that could have otherwise killed the warrior. It was indeed a necessary tool in battle.

The Word of God promises that our tools for warfare are essential in our ability to fight, even when it is a spiritual war! Even though we know we have an eternal home with God in Heaven, while we are on this earth, we are forever fighting against the evil one, that old devil, the one we know as Satan.

Open your Bible and read Ephesians 6:11-18. In that passage we see:

> "Put on the whole armour of God, that ye may be able to stand against the wiles of the devil. 12 For we wrestle not against flesh and blood, but against principalities, against powers, against the rulers of the darkness of this world, against spiritual wickedness in high places. 13 Wherefore take unto you the whole armour of God, that ye may be able to withstand in the evil day, and having done all, to stand. 14 Stand therefore, having your loins girt about with truth, and having on the breastplate of righteousness; 15 And your feet shod with the preparation of the gospel of peace; 16 Above all, taking the shield of faith, wherewith ye shall be able to quench all the fiery darts of the wicked. 17 And take the helmet of salvation, and the sword of the Spirit, which is the word of God: 18 Praying always with all prayer and supplication in the Spirit, and watching thereunto with all perseverance and supplication for all saints"

We see in verses 14 and 15 that we have the shield of faith and the breastplate of righteousness. This is our buckler! Are you prepared for battle? When you are daily in the Word you can rely upon what you know to be the truth that sets you free. And you are confident that the Lord is ever with you. All glory to Him!

UPRIGHTNESS OF HEART

Key Bible Passage: Psalms 119:6-7a Then shall I not be ashamed, when I have respect unto all thy commandments. I will praise thee with uprightness of heart…

All of us have experienced embarrassment sometime in our life. It could be something as simple as a split seam in the clothes we are wearing or forgetting to lock the bathroom door and an unexpected visitor walks in. Even worse, is when we discover that everyone else knows about it.

However, being embarrassed is not quite the same as being ashamed. Being ashamed is usually caused by something we did or failed to do that led to the disapproval of someone else we respect. Or, in some cases, we were doing something we should not be doing. Likewise, there must have been an expectation of what we were supposed to do or not do, and we failed to do the right thing.

Our key Bible passage speaks to our attitude when it comes to God's directives in our life. When we respect what God has to say to us, it causes us not to be ashamed. The word ashamed is not used as much today as it was used many years ago. In fact, some would say that there has been a loss of shame in our culture when it comes to some of the outrageous behaviors that are tolerated today.

For example, there was a time when we did not use foul language and cursing around others, much less children. But you can now walk down the halls of elementary schools and hear eight-year-old children using the most extreme of filthy language. This is because they were never taught to have respect for others in the way that they speak. When their parents do not demonstrate respect for others in the way they speak, the children learn to disrespect others from what their parents have modeled.

When it comes to being ashamed Biblically, we can be ashamed before God. Yet, it takes on a deeper meaning in that He teaches that we can be ashamed even when we go through tough times.

However, He promises that through our time of tribulation He will teach us patience, give us experience, and give us hope. Hope then makes us not to be ashamed (Romans 5:3-5). In this context, when we are ashamed before God, it is demonstrated in our lack of confidence to step out fearlessly in faith.

Therefore, when we realize that we are in a situation where we do the wrong thing, or we do not know how to handle it, we need to bring our concerns to the Lord in prayer.

If we have done wrong, we need to confess our sin, and God will cleanse us of all unrighteousness. When we lack confidence in knowing what to do, we must submit our requests to God in prayer with supplication and thanksgiving. In doing so, He will guard our hearts and minds and reestablish our uprightness and confidence.

Finally, the result of this is that we will no longer be ashamed. But instead, we will confidently and openly praise Him out of the wellspring of our heart, which He has reestablished to be a light in a dark world. Let us therefore consider how we respect God's commandments and our standing before Him. Let us actively seek His intervention in our heart. We can then be confident that He will set our hearts upright again and we can praise Him before the world in all that we say and do.

NEW TEMPLE FOUNDATION

Key Bible Passage: Matthew 7:24–25
Therefore whosoever heareth these sayings of mine, and doeth them, I will liken him unto a wise man, which built his house upon a rock: And the rain descended, and the floods came, and the winds blew, and beat upon that house; and it fell not: for it was founded upon a rock.

Many Christians refer to the local church as the "house of God." In fact, over the years many people were raised being taught that when you are in church that you should speak softly, dress a certain way, and be respectful of the time of worship. This teaching is often based on a historical practice and reflective of a time when people in general were more reverent in all things pertaining to the tenets of our faith.

The Old Testament is very clear about the respect and honor toward the activities and practices that took place at the temple. There were hundreds of prescribed ways of performing the duties of a priest and assuring that reverence, respect, and honor were maintained. Of most importance was the fact that the Shekinah Glory of God inhabited the Holy of Holies, the place where God abode amongst humanity. Unfortunately, it was only the High Priest that was allowed into His presence during a certain prescribed time of the year.

With the coming of the New Testament, Jesus demonstrated the Old Testament laws and teachings were more than just rules of behavior but were also matters of the heart. When discussing adultery, He preached that not only was it literally wrong, but pondering the same in our heart made us just as guilty. Likewise, He said the same about murder, that just being angry with someone in our heart without just cause was also murder. Overall, Jesus made the law more relatable to us as humans in that when we fully apply the law to our heart, not just our deeds, all of us fall short of the glory of God.

It is the same when it comes to the house of God. God demonstrated this truth when He tore the curtain separating the Holy Place from the Most Holy Place at the very moment Jesus died on the cross for our sins. In doing so, He demonstrated that direct access to the very presence of God was no longer limited to the High Priest. No longer were sins addressed through the death of animals offered by human priests mediating for us with God. More importantly, God revealed that He was no longer there, living in a house of wood and stone made with human hands. This act of God literally shook the very foundations of the earth.

In like manner, God now offers us a more perfect sacrifice: holy, perfect, and complete through the death, burial, and resurrection of our eternal High Priest, Jesus Christ. He provides the foundation for a new temple and Holy of Holies for God to live in our hearts. Let us prayerfully consider how we behave in our new House of God by standing on the Rock of a new Foundation, Jesus Christ. He will inspire and enable us to speak softly to others and put off the former curtain of selfishness and pride. He will inspire and enable us to put on a new curtain, opened by the hand of God for all to see, of selfless service and love toward others where the storms of life will never shake its firm foundation.

THE LOVE OF LEARNING

Key Bible Passage: Psalms 119:7b-8 ...when I shall have learned thy righteous judgments. I will keep thy statutes: O forsake me not utterly.

There is nothing quite like the joy and wonder of a newborn baby. From that first moment when he or she opens their eyes to the day they take their first steps; every day is a learning experience. At the same time, while they grow physically and socially, the person they spend the most time with is looked to for comfort, provision, and learning.

As parents, we are engrained with a natural desire to want the best for our children. We invest the time and effort to teach them and guide them so that they grow up to be strong and independent and prepared for the day when they go out into the world to make their own way. While doing this, we will notice that while they may or may not look like us, good or bad, we will notice that they will begin to act like us. This is because, as their teacher, we have great influence over who they become.

No matter whom it is, anyone that spends time learning from someone else becomes more like their teacher. As parent-teachers, this is important to keep in mind. As we diligently teach and model things that we want for our children, they will become what we want them to be. However, if we do not invest the time and effort to teach and model the same, they will turn to someone else and become like them.

God teaches us as His children through His Word. As parents we must then take the time to immerse our children in His Word. From the moment they get up, go out, go to school, go home, and go to bed, we must talk about what God says and demonstrate what God wants. Every moment must be made a learning opportunity to fill their hearts and minds with the love of Christ. However, before we can do this for our children, we must be willing to do this ourselves (Deuteronomy 6:4-9).

Our key Bible passage continues the thought from the previous passage in that when we respect God's commandments, we shall not be ashamed and praise Him with uprightness of heart. This uprightness of heart inspires us to want to learn God's righteous judgments in all aspects of our life. Then, as parents when we have those special times and close moments with our children and we openly share our hearts, they will see the genuine love that we have for God and for them.

Furthermore, when we make the effort to do this, we implant or write the same on their hearts. This prepares their hearts to receive the truth of the gospel of Jesus Christ. The truth that He was crucified and died for our sins, was buried, and rose again on the third day. When they receive this truth and believe it, they are then given the gift of the Holy Spirit from God, Whom empowers and inspires them. Then they, like us, will be motivated to keep God's statutes and seek His approval in every aspect of their life.

Let us devote time daily with our Father, allowing Him to share His heart and desires for our lives. Let us demonstrate our love of learning from Him and what He did by following His teaching in our lives. Then we, and our children can learn with full assurance that He has not forsaken us, but instead wants His very best for us.

NOISE OF JOY

Key Bible Passage: Psalms 81:1-2 "Sing aloud unto God our strength: make a joyful noise unto the God of Jacob. Take a psalm, and bring hither the timbrel, the pleasant harp with the psaltery."

When I read this Psalm, I was immediately reminded of how I learned as a young child that when you sing to the Lord you are praying twice. The Lord loves to hear us sing and He has even given us many, many musical instruments to help us as we praise His Holy Name. I found quite a few of these instruments in the Bible. Take a look at how we can make "Noise of Joy" on these beautiful tools.

In today's verse we see mention of the timbrel. This is a word we don't hear so much anymore. Did you know a tambourine is another name for the timbrel? You can also see this percussion instrument mentioned in Exodus 15:20, Judges 11:34, 2 Samuel 6:5, 1 Chronicles 13:8, Job 21:12 as well as in 3 other Psalms.

We also see mention of the harp, which I think we all know is an upright or handheld instrument of strings. And then we see the psaltery, which is another ancient string instrument, much like today's dulcimer. In addition to the harp and psaltery we see sackbut, with only four strings in the shape of a triangle (Daniel 3:5). We also see it called a lyre or a trigon.

Other instruments include the many horns like the trumpet (Joshua 6:4), and the shofar which was used to get people's attention or to call people to prayer (Joshua 6;20, 1 Kings 1:34, Job 39:24, more) and just plain "horn": (Hosea 5:8).

You can also find the flute, pipes (bagpipes) and the organ mentioned. Many times, we will even see the organ referred to as "pipes" (Genesis 4:21, Psalms 150:1-6, 1 Samuel 10:5, Isaiah 30:29, Daniel 3:5, Job 21:12, more).

Certainly, there is no shortage of percussion in the Bible as well. Many times, that was the only instrument used. We see instances of previously mentioned timbrel or tambourine as well as the drum (Psalms 150:4-5). And perhaps the noisiest of the percussion where the cymbals; those used on fingers and later larger ones that were brought together with the hands (1 Chronicles 15:28, Psalms 150:5, 1 Corinthians 13:1,).

And finally, we all have an instrument with our voice. Whether or not you have the voice of an angel or sound like a dog howling at the moon, when the Lord hears you sing, it is a joyful noise! God is our strength and praising Him with our voice and on other musical instruments is how we were made to worship. Raise your voice or raise your other instrument and give Him the glory and honor because He is worthy of no less than our best!

WAYWARD WANDERING

Key Bible Passage: Psalms 119:9-10
Wherewithal shall a young man cleanse his way? by taking heed thereto according to thy word. With my whole heart have I sought thee: O let me not wander from thy commandments.

So you ever have one of those moments when you are trying to do something and there is something that you need to get it done? So, you stop what you are doing, to get that thing, but along the way someone or something distracts you. You deal with the distraction, but now you've forgotten what you came to get in the first place! (I know, some of us do not even need a distraction to forget what we were looking for.) So, we go back to what we were doing to figure out what we needed in the first place.

In today's world, we find that our lives are full of distractions. It may be work, or school, our children, or even the race to get things done during the week. Then add to that the distractions of social media, politics, or even trouble within our family. Before long we find that we struggle just keeping it all together much less having time to spend making things better in our own lives.

Our key Bible passage asks the question, *"Wherewithal shall a young man cleanse his ways?"* In other words, by what means or how does he do this? The answer is *"by taking heed thereto according to thy Word."* It is by paying attention and listening to what God's Word has to say about it. In the context of being distracted, we need to focus on what God tells us about it. This focus is then an important factor to consider if we seek to cleanse our way.

In our previous devotions, we explored the role and position that our heart plays in setting our direction and motivating us to follow what God has commanded us to do. When we combine this with taking heed to the specifics that address cleansing our way then we develop a hunger to seek God more and more with each passing day. In turn, this opens our eyes to areas in our lives that need our attention. At the same time, the things that distract us become less distracting so that we are not easily distracted from seeking God with our whole heart. This causes our faith to increase even more.

God teaches us that faith is the substance of things hoped for; the evidence of things not seen (Hebrews 11:1). The substance of things hoped for is the faith that we have in what Christ did for us on the cross to save us. His love for us to do this motivates us to want to learn more about Him and causes us to want to seek Him with our whole heart. As we do this, He changes our heart, and we start seeing changes in our desires and ways of doing things. This change excites us as we see that this fruit of a changed life is not of our doing, but of His doing. Instead of being distracted by the world and doing things our way, we are then focused and led by His Spirit to do things His way – a way that is clean, and pure, and holy. We then call out to God to take over our lives so that we no longer are distracted by our own wayward wandering.

Let us consider our ways and ask if they are full of distractions and detours from what God wants for us. Let us be devoted to spending time in God's Word. In doing so, God will bless us with a changed heart and the ability to see the clear path, void of distraction, leading us to doing right.

RESTFUL REST

Key Bible Passage: Matthew 11:28–29 Come unto me, all ye that labour and are heavy laden, and I will give you rest. Take my yoke upon you, and learn of me; for I am meek and lowly in heart: and ye shall find rest unto your souls.

Rest, we all need it, but do we all get it? How many times have you laid your head to rest only to find that you toss and turn rather than really rest? You know you have had good rest when you wake, and you feel refreshed and rejuvenated. But did you truly get "restful rest".

This "restful rest" of which I speak is the rest that you can get only from the Sleep Master the One whom created rest for Himself first: *"And on the seventh day God ended his work which he had made; and he rested on the seventh day from all his work which he had made"* (Genesis 2:2)

This rest set a pattern for us. We work and then we rest. We lay our weary body down and it drifts into a slumber, healing sore muscles and even sore brain cells. This is a good rest, and it is a necessary rest, but even so, it is not that "restful rest".

The Key Bible Passage today is one that is familiar to many. It reminds us that Jesus wants us to give Him our burdens and it promises that He will give us rest. He offers us His yoke so that we might learn from Him. This "yoke" refers to the burden of the law. He is offering Himself as the Master and inviting us to follow him. Following Jesus only has to happen once. When we follow Him, we no longer have to keep all of those old commandments. When we keep our eyes upon Him, we will do what pleases Him. It is no longer about keeping the letter of the law, but now it is about believing that He is the fulfillment of that law! In this, our burden to keep the law becomes light because Jesus already did everything we need to become righteous. We no longer need to work our way to become acceptable to God in our own self-righteous ways. We no longer need to carry the burden of the law.

God promises to go before us and give us rest (Exodus 33:14). We are encouraged to rest and sleep in the LORD (Psalms 4:8; 37:7). He leads us, restores us, keeps us safe and feeds us (Psalms 23).

We can have that "restful rest" and it is found only in Jesus. We are reminded and promised that rest by the writer of Hebrews *"There remaineth therefore a rest to the people of God. For he that is entered into his rest, he also hath ceased from his own works, as God did from his. Let us labour therefore to enter into that rest, lest any man fall after the same example of unbelief."* (Hebrews 4:9-11)

Lord! M*9ake us to see that we need Jesus. Help us to get that "restful rest" that only He gives. Draw us to love Your word and seek to meditate upon it throughout the day. And mostly Lord, give us a grateful heart and prompt us to tell others about our good night's sleep – Your "restful rest".

HIDE AND GO SEEK

Key Bible Passage: Psalms 119:11-12 Thy word have I hid in mine heart, that I might not sin against thee. Blessed art thou, O LORD: teach me thy statutes.

A fun game for kids is the game Hide and Go Seek. Generally, the game is started when someone is selected to be "it", and they have to hide their eyes and count to a number like 100 while all the others go find a place to hide. When the person is finished counting, they call out, "Ready or not, here I come!" and then go look for the others that are hiding. The first person they find is "it" for the next round while the last person found is the winner.

A good Hide and Go Seek player looks for a hiding place that is hard to find and offers the maximum amount of concealment. They hide in the deepest reaches of their hiding place so that they cannot be easily seen. The person that is "it" must then look hard to find out where they are hidden.

Our Key Bible Passage tells us about hiding God's Word in our heart. In the context of previous passages, doing this has an effect on us in that it changes our heart. Our changed, or upright heart, then serves as a basis from which God changes our lives. However, to change our lives we must know what is in our heart and what needs changed. Furthermore, when it comes to knowing our heart, who is doing the searching and what will they find? This question in life leads many of us to want to go to great lengths to "find our self."

The problem with seeking to find our self is that our expectation and ability to know where to look and recognize who we are or accept what we find does not match reality. Instead, our expectation matches what we hope we will find. When our expectation does not match reality, it causes unsettled angst and trouble in our minds. Like the person that is "it" in Hide and Go Seek, we then look from place to place hoping to find someone that is not there.

The question we have to ask is, "Who is "it?" Are we "it", hopelessly and blindly searching for someone we do not know? Or, is God "It" because He has the vision and ability to understand where to look and knows who He will find? Fortunately, the Bible teaches us that God can see into the deepest reaches of our heart and can test us to show who we really are (Jeremiah 17:9-10). His expectations are based on reality of what is, not our hope of what we are. Therefore, as we hide God's Word in our heart, it measures us against God's standards, not our own. It reveals who we are and where we are hiding with the light of His holiness.

This is because as God, His Word is active and alive and sharper than any two-edged sword. It is able to divide our soul and spirit from the very joints and marrow of our bodies. It is a discerner of the thoughts and intents of our heart, revealing to us who we really are. It enables us to change so that we live up to God's standards and see God as the "It" in our lives Whom puts an end to our constant hiding and go seeking of self.

Let us pray that God examines our heart and teaches us who we are and what He wants us to be. Let us seek an unhidden openness before the Lord as He blesses us and teaches us His statutes. In doing so, instead of giving up when we cannot find our self, we can call out to God, Blessed art thou O LORD for finding me! Praise be to God Whom makes us all winners.

SEEKING AND GETTING

Key Bible Passage: Proverbs 18:15 The heart of the prudent getteth knowledge; And the ear of the wise seeketh knowledge.

Not long ago I was blessed to carry on a conversation with a dear sister in Christ whom has lived a long life. I wanted to share with her my thoughts and beliefs but before I knew it, she was sharing so much with me that I could not help but just sit there and listen. I realized she had so many years of life experience that had taught her things that I had yet to learn.

As she spoke her words were careful and discreet. She was reasonable and discerning. As she shared true stories from her life I learned of her shrewdness and excellent economic sense. Her heart and lifestyle were frugal and sound, and she not only sought knowledge, but she also obtained it as well. When I look for a definition of "prudent" I consider this dear sister to be the epitome of just that!

Today's Key Bible Passage comes from a chapter in Proverbs that many overlook. Like many of the other Proverbs, when we read this chapter, we can see how the foolish man is compared and contrasted to the wise man. For example, when we look back in this chapter to Proverbs 18:2 we see *"A fool has no delight in understanding, but that his heart may discover itself"*. The fool has no desire to "seek" knowledge outside of himself. He believes that everything he needs is within "himself". He may believe that he has all of the answers to life and when he searches within himself, he will have a "Eureka" moment. He might believe that he can make positive things happen, just because he thinks it to be so.

Don't misunderstand me, I do believe the Bible teaches that we should think on good things and refrain from thinking on those things that are not good (read also Philippians 4:6-9). However, the Bible does not teach that we can have wisdom and knowledge in and of ourselves.

Wisdom and knowledge are great mysteries of life, and they are great treasures. These treasures are given by God and hidden in Christ (1 Corinthians 1:24-28; Colossians 2:2-3). So then, God grants us wisdom and knowledge too when we are "in Christ". You are "in Christ" when you have accepted Jesus' sacrifice as payment for your sin – this is the moment of salvation. Before you were "in

Christ" you were an enemy of God (Romans 5:10). But the good news is that at that moment of salvation Jesus takes our list of sins upon Himself and gives us His perfect account which makes us pleasing to God. God offers wisdom and knowledge to all so that we might not glory in our own flesh but rather glory in the Lord because in Christ Jesus *"God is made unto us wisdom, and righteousness, and sanctification and redemption"* (1 Corinthians 1:30-31)

Lord, help us to seek You and Your wisdom. Show us in Your Word and in other believers how to get knowledge. Help us to get outside of our self and rest in Jesus as our true source of wisdom and knowledge. And once we understand the things of You, give us the desire to teach others, so that they might also want to seek and get You.

TESTIFYING OF TRUTH

Key Bible Passage: Psalms 119:13-14 With my lips have I declared all the judgments of thy mouth. I have rejoiced in the way of thy testimonies, as much as in all riches.

Some of the most popular shows on television are those that involve crime and justice. The shows typically start with a crime being committed and the audience follows along while law enforcement officers solve the case, and it goes to trial. At trial, witnesses tell their stories of what happened and by the conclusion of the show a verdict is made.

It is interesting that some people will say that art imitates life. They claim, what we see in art reflects what we see in life. Crime shows demonstrate this in that they have twists and turns that leave the viewer on the edge of their seat. Witnesses tell conflicting stories; suspects have politically incorrect agendas; and each side seeks verdicts that promote their version of how the law should be. Gone are the days when the person being charged breaks down and confesses they broke the law.

Sadly, we also see these changes in real life. People are charged with high profile crimes and prosecutors have to thread their way through a minefield of true and false witnesses to discover the truth. Decisions are rejected because those with no knowledge or regard for the facts accuse the authorities of bias or misconduct because they did not believe someone's "version" of the truth.

Our Key Bible Passage teaches us about the value of speaking the truth. It demonstrates that when we declare or "testify" of God's judgments and testimonies we should do so with rejoicing like we would if we were suddenly endowed with riches. More specifically, what we say and do should be a direct result of God's testimony.

God teaches us that His Word is truth. Jesus reinforced this as God when He said, *"I am the way, the truth and the life"* (John 14:6). He also told of the power and truth of God's Word in saying, *"Sanctify them through thy truth: thy word is truth"* (John 17:17). Therefore, as believers, it is important that we look to God's Word as our source of truth. It is important that we seek God's testimony in all the affairs of life. When we do this, we can then rejoice in the fact that the judgments of the Lord can be relied upon. Therefore, when we speak of

God's judgments with our mouth, we can be sure that what we testify to is the truth. It is this truth that proves to be more valuable than riches. This truth is powerful, and eternal, and can be relied upon for making sound judgments in all the matters of life.

Let us pray that we stay focused on God's testimonies and not the testimonies of the world. Let us consider that when any topic or subject is discussed, we should be bold witnesses of the truth that God says about the matter. Let us consider that although the opinions of many may drive public conversations and direction, it is the truth of God's Word that needs to be spoken at the right time. Let us be bold in leaving a Godly testimony in all that we say and do. Let us preach the Word in the right context, doing the work of an evangelist: reproving, rebuking, and testifying of the riches of God's Wisdom as manifested in Christ as His living Word. Praise be to God!

SET YOUR EYES UPON IT

Key Bible Passage: Proverbs 23:5 Wilt thou set thine eyes upon that which is not? for riches certainly make themselves wings; they fly away as an eagle toward heaven.

Have you ever wanted something so bad for so long and then when you finally got it you were somewhat disappointed? This has happened to me. I thought about this particular car that I wanted. Before I wanted the car, I almost never saw another like it. Then when the thought of having that car was constantly on my mind, I saw similar ones all over the roadways. I "set my eyes upon" that car and for some time it was not within my reach. I not only set my eyes upon it, but I also believe it qualified as something that I coveted.

And then it happened, that day when I was able to get that car. Oh! It was so pretty and new. I drove it to and from my workplace every day. But you know what? It was not long before I realized that this car, on which I spent so much time dreaming about, and in which I spent so much time sitting – this car was terribly uncomfortable! So, then I started thinking about a time when I might get a car that was more comfortable. I was ready to get rid of that "old" car.

When I read today's verse I thought of that car because I remembered how I "set my eyes upon it". And then after I got it, it was not long before I was ready to see it go. Easy come, easy go. That is exactly what happens with our treasures (riches) here on earth. They are only temporary and in light of eternity, they make themselves wings and then we have them no more.

I was also reminded of something Jesus said that we should not lay up treasures on earth because they don't last long, but instead our treasure should be in heaven because heavenly things are not temporary (Matthew 6:19-24). Now this is not to say that we cannot enjoy the fruit of our labor, but when we spend more time and resource on earthly "things" than we do on the work of the Lord our priorities are out of order.

As Christ-followers the main "riches" that we should set our eyes upon are other people who need to hear the truth of the gospel of Jesus Christ - we need to spend time sharing the greatest news we have ever learned. There is no greater gift, no greater treasure than the gift of grace. Have you told anyone about your Savior today? Selah

SACRIFICE OF SELF

Key Bible Passage: Psalms 119:15-16
I will meditate in thy precepts, and have respect unto thy ways. I will delight myself in thy statutes: I will not forget thy word.

A popular activity in many areas of the world is Yoga. Yoga is a type of worship practiced by Hindus and some others that is mentioned in Hindu texts as far back as 800-600 B.C. It involves deep meditation to extinguish or liberate one's soul from rebirth and attain spiritual oneness with Brahman, a Hindu god of absolute reality within each person. This extinguishing or sacrifice of self in meditation is called Nirvana.

Westerners have added a more pronounced exercise component to Yoga with claims of health benefits. However, the goal remains to empty one's self in search of finding a purified version of self that is in tune with nature or the universe. In the end, the meditation is focused on emptying the mind.

Our Key Bible Passage presents to us a different concept when it comes to meditation. It focuses on filling our minds with His way of thinking as it relates to our self as individuals. Minimizing self does not sacrifice our humanity, but instead seeks to allow God to change us to be more like His Son, Jesus Christ, whom was fully God and fully man.

As a man, Jesus encountered all the trials and struggles that we do. However, He taught us that He could do nothing by or for Himself, rather He always did those things that pleased the Father. Therefore, instead of emptying Himself, He taught us through His example, to change to be more like Him. The way we do this is not for us to seek to sacrifice who we are, but instead to meditate upon God's sacrifice and precepts so that He changes us to be more like who He is. God does this because He loves us and wants to have a good relationship with us. As humans, God designed us to be social beings with personalities, not empty shells of energy that cannot have relationships.

Seeing this positive change in our lives inspires us to have respect for God's ways. We find delight in God's statutes because of our love for Him and because of what Jesus did for us when He died on the cross for our sins. We see Jesus as a common example of how we should be as individuals. As we study God's

Word and learn more about Jesus and His love for us, His Word becomes hidden in our hearts.

When we experience different life situations, God's Holy Spirit brings to remembrance Bible passages for us to use in guiding our ways. When we see the effects of these passages, we respect God's ways more and more with each passing day. Therefore, our goal of meditation is not to extinguish our self, but to fill our minds with those things that He wants us to be.

Let us consider that our goal in meditation is to meditate on what God says in His Word. Our goal is to also see ourselves as unique individuals with gifts and talents that God wants us to use in relationships to serve others. Our goal is to use these relationships to share the love of God through giving of our self on a personal level, not an impersonal one. Finally, our goal is for all of us to learn to love God and others as our self. Praise be to God!

THE GOOD AND PERFECT GIFT

Key Bible Passage: James 1:17 Every good gift and every perfect gift is from above, and cometh down from the Father of lights, with whom is no variableness, neither shadow of turning.

Nearly everyone likes to receive a gift. Whether it is something practical or something that is just plain fun. The giver of the gift often puts a lot of thought and consideration into the gift that they want to give. When it comes to God our Father, He knows every hair on our head, and He knows every concern and desire of our heart. So, when He chose to provide us a gift, He wanted one that would be perfect and that would fulfill the desires of our heart that we do not know we even have.

God knew that the gift He would give us must be a good gift - one that is perfect. The gift that God chose for us was Himself in the form of His Son, Jesus Christ. Born as a baby and growing into a man, Jesus was given unto us to provide for the greatest need of each and every one of us - the need to have an eternal close relationship with God the Father.

However, in our natural state we cannot have that because our human sins and imperfections prevent us from being in the very presence of a good and perfect Father. This is not to say that God does not want to be near us unless we are perfect. It simply means that He wants to provide a way for it to happen by first making us good and perfect like Him.

Therefore, Jesus lived a good and perfect life for us and allowed Himself to be wrongfully crucified so that He could pay our penalty for our sins and imperfections, which is death and eternal separation from God. This was His gift to us, saving us from our penalty by giving us His goodness and perfection. Furthermore, He made it so that when we trust in what He did for us to provide His gift of salvation, we also receive Him into our lives in the form of God the Holy Spirit to live inside us. There, He provides for our practical needs and gives us joy and peace beyond all understanding. This motivates us to love God and others because He first loved us.

Let us accept God's calling to draw near to Him by trusting in His Son Jesus Christ as the good and perfect gift of God. The gift that provides for every need and gives us the peace and the joy and comfort that God, our eternal Father, so desires that each of us have.

TRANSGRESSION OF THE LAW

Key Bible Passage: 1 John 3:4 Whosoever committeth sin transgresseth also the law: for sin is the transgression of the law.

Transgression...now that's a big word. Ask a student to define it for you and what will you get? "I don't know". Okay then, let's pick a simpler, smaller word. Ask a student to define the word "sin" for you. Nine times out of ten you will get exactly the same answer: "I don't know". Why? Because it is a word that most people just don't use any more today.

Sin is a word that, just twenty years ago, was a regular part of our vocabulary. And more than fifty years ago the definition of sin was still taught in our schools, before we removed the Bible. It is a Biblical word and when you look it up in the Webster's Dictionary from 1828 the definition includes words like "...sin is either a positive act in which a known divine law is violated, or it is the voluntary neglect to obey a positive divine command, or a rule of duty clearly implied in such command. sin comprehends not action only, but neglect of known duty, all evil thoughts purposes, words and desires, whatever is contrary to God's commands or law."

Well, there you go, that 1828 definition speaks of "God's commands or law" and now we can unpack the meaning of "transgression of the law". Simply put, "transgression" is a violation of a law. So then, "sin" and "transgression" are really the same thing.

The Key Bible Passage today was shared by the apostle John. John continues in this chapter to teach that the law helps us to know that we are sinful (Romans 3:20). And because of sin we all come short of the glory of God (Romans 3:23). But the good news is that God gave us a remedy. His name is Jesus, and He was given by God the Father to pay our sin debt. He willingly allowed Himself to be wrongfully crucified on the cross as our substitute. When we believe in what He did for us on that cross our sin debt is marked "paid in full". And even better yet, when we believe this God also gives us His Holy Spirit to indwell us and lead us in the right way. He, the Holy Spirit, guides us along in life and gives us choices that help us to do what pleases the Lord. When we make the good choices, we do not sin, and we do not transgress the law. This is the only way to keep from committing sin because when our eyes are on Jesus instead of on the things of this world, we will do right. You see while we are on earth it is impossible to be sinless, but when we keep our eyes upon Jesus it is possible to sin less!

Lord, we need your perfect Sinless Son Jesus to lead us in the right way. Help us to follow Him and the Holy Spirit so that we might not transgress. Inspire us to teach our children the meaning of these Biblical terms "sin" and "transgression". Motivate us to help our children to fall in love with Jesus before they are old enough to make the choice to fall in love with the world. Urge us to make Bible reading and study an important part of our daily family time. Make us to remember You and think of You from the time we get out of bed until the time we lay back to sleep.

TRIBULATIONS, BITTER OR BETTER?

Key Bible Passage: Romans 6:14-16 For sin shall not have dominion over you: for ye are not under the law, but under grace. What then? shall we sin, because we are not under the law, but under grace? God forbid.

We live in a time when it seems like everyone believes they are a victim of someone or something. Unfortunately, even Christians fall into this mindset. As believers are we destined to be victims while we live on this earth?

It is no secret that each of us were born into a world that is in constant conflict and turmoil. This is because the world is saturated with the effects of sin that were unleashed by Satan that fateful day in the garden. This saturation of sin is so complete that it has permeated all aspects of creation so that not only do we suffer, but all creation groans under its weight.

We must remember that just as God has delivered us from the deadliness or our sins by His grace, He has also made us able to be impermeable to sin in our daily lives. The power of sin to penetrate us, dominate us, and cause bitterness in our lives has been destroyed. The father of sin has been defeated. His kingdom does not rule over us anymore. We are not of his world anymore. Yet many of us, as believers, walk around bitter at God and everyone else because we live with the mindset that Satan is still our abusive father. In doing so, we allow Satan to have an opening through the impermeable protection that God has provided to us. Satan then takes this opening and uses it to wreak havoc and bitterness in our lives.

We must remember that by God's grace we were saved and by God's grace we are able to boldly step forward not as victims, but as victors. Therefore, let us glory in our tribulations because it is only by tribulations that we have opportunities to exercise our faith to grow stronger. Tribulations also show us that Satan does not like what we have done in becoming a child of God. So, we must use these tribulations as opportunities to exercise our faith, and teach us patience, which gives us experience. As we witness the power of God work through these experiences, we gain hope, an anchor for the soul, that motivates us and sustains us in even the worst of times.

We must always keep in mind that while we were yet sinners, without power to live our lives as victors, Christ died for us. We were reborn into His family, sealed until the day of redemption, and given the power to walk in newness of life by the Holy Spirit, Whom has now permeated us to our very soul, displacing the sin that so easily besets us. Therefore, let us always remember that the tribulations of this world should not make us bitter, they should make us better.

GOD'S BOUNTIFUL PROVISION

Key Bible Passage: Psalms 119:17
Deal bountifully with thy servant, that I may live, and keep thy word.

Many artists have drawn or painted a bowl or basket of fruit. Around Thanksgiving, the fruit and even vegetables are staged as a decoration so that they appear to be spilling out of a horn shaped basket. The basket, called a cornucopia, or horn of plenty, originated in Greek mythology as a goat's horn filled with milk, and later grains and nuts, to feed the Greek god Zeus.

The word cornucopia combines the words cornu, meaning horn (like in coronet), and copia (like in copious), meaning abundant. This thinking led to it being used as a table decoration in times of harvest to symbolize the never-ending provision of an abundant harvest.

Our key Bible passage addresses the hope that God would deal bountifully with us as His servants. As servants, God has called us to do His work. At the same time, God knows that we may need things to accomplish what He wants us to do. For example, if God calls us to feed the hungry, He knows we may need things such as food; containers to store, prepare, or serve it; cooking utensils; and a place to cook and serve the food.

The wonderful thing about God's calling is that when it is the Lord's will, He will make a way. If we think about it, God never had to take out a mortgage to fund the creation of the heavens and the earth. Likewise, God never has to rely on us to accomplish what He wants done. This does not mean that we sit back and say, "Okay God, work your magic. Show me what you got!" Instead, God wants us to be a willing part of His plan: not to see what we can get, but to see what we can give as a demonstration of our love for Him.

However, we must also keep in mind that despite our best efforts, God can always provide for a harvest that is beyond anything we could ever produce on our own. This means that no matter what our part is in the planting and watering, it is God who provides the bountiful and abundant increase for us to harvest. Likewise, God will provide for our living while we carry out His calling.

Just like the lowly ox that does his part in plowing, and planting, and sowing, God provides for his physical needs, and He will provide for ours (1 Timothy 5:18). Furthermore, He also provides the power, ability, and wisdom we need to do what He has called us to do (1 Corinthians 1:24-31).

Let us consider that with God's will and power and might and wisdom, we can have the mind of Christ to do all things through Him to keep His Word in our hearts and minds. When we are able to keep His Word in our hearts and minds, it provides a lamp unto our feet and a light unto our path so that we may live to fulfill His calling. When we live to fulfill His calling, we can be eyewitnesses of His majesty and see the full bounty of His provision in everything around us.

Finally, let us make a joyful noise unto the Lord and serve Him with gladness. For He is God and has made us to be His people and the sheep of His pasture. Let us then enter His courts of public opinion with thanksgiving and praise: thankful unto Him and His blessed name. For He is good, and His mercy is everlasting and endures to all generations. Praise be to God!

TRY ME AND KNOW MY THOUGHTS

Key Bible Passage: 1 Samuel 16:7 But the Lord said unto Samuel, Look not on his countenance, or on the height of his stature; because I have refused him: for the Lord seeth not as man seeth; for man looketh on the outward appearance, but the Lord looketh on the heart.

This verse in 1 Samuel chapter 16 comes right after the LORD rejects the evil King Saul from reigning over Israel. In the previous chapter He used Samuel (a judge) to announce to Saul that he was rejected because he was rebellious and obeyed not the LORD's voice. This was very hard on Samuel, and he received chastisement from the LORD who told him to basically quit complaining and get busy to find another king.

As the LORD would have it, He let Samuel in on His plan when He sent Samuel to see Jesse the Beth-lehemite because the new king was among Jesse's sons (1 Samuel 16:1). But Samuel was afraid Saul would kill him as he traveled to do the LORD's will. Even so, he went and of course the LORD protected Samuel as he went to Bethlehem.

Samuel met with Jesse and immediately believed that the first born of his sons, Eliab, was the one the LORD chose to replace Saul. But he was wrong, and it was not until Jesse saw each of the seven sons that the LORD revealed that the chosen one was, in fact, the youngest, a young and little shepherd boy named David.

It was not David's size or strength that made the LORD choose David, it was David's heart that the LORD loved. Samuel could not see what the LORD saw.

Isn't this true even today? Don't we judge a book by its cover? Don't we sometimes totally get it wrong? We often mistake a lovely meek person as a weak person. We even sometimes choose to follow a person because they have much confidence and when they walk in the room, they appear to control it all. Only later to learn that they were so full of themselves that they were not a wise choice at all.

God sees it all. We can run but we cannot hide from Him (Genesis 3:8-10; Jeremiah 23:24). He knows every hair on our head (Luke 12:7). He knows our thoughts (Matthew 12:25; Luke 6:8). And he knows are heart too. Are you happy with what God sees in your heart?

Can you ask what the psalmist asked in Psalm 139:23-24: *"Search me, O God, and know my heart: Try me, and know my thoughts: 24 And see if there be any wicked way in me, And lead me in the way everlasting"*? Oh! That we could humble our self before the LORD and then follow where He leads.

CHOOSE THE GOOD FRUIT

Key Bible Passage Galatians 5:22-23 But the fruit of the Spirit is love, joy, peace, longsuffering, gentleness, goodness, faith, Meekness, temperance: against such there is no law.

Anyone who likes fruit generally likes it to be fresh fruit. For example, wouldn't you much rather have some pineapple that was cut fresh and served to you than to have it out of a can? I know I would! The fact of the matter is that there is good fruit and there is bad fruit. Fruit that has been left out in the sun too long will spoil and stink. It has been exposed to that thing that continues to make it turn rotten and undesirable.

In today's Bible verse Paul talks about fruit. This is that familiar passage in Scripture that reminds us that the Holy Spirit's influence in our life produces "good" fruit. This fruit is the outward sign that He is in control, and we are not afraid to let Him have control. He continually produces this good fruit and if we are listening to and following Him, we can have a life that is abundant even here on earth.

Just prior to this passage in the Bible Paul was talking about the things that are a product of a life spent ignoring good and choosing to follow fleshly desires. These are the works of the flesh:

"Now the works of the flesh are manifest, which are these; Adultery, fornication, uncleanness, lasciviousness, Idolatry, witchcraft, hatred, variance, emulations, wrath, strife, seditions, heresies," (Galatians 5:19-20)

Paul was admonishing the Christians that were at Galatia because they were "biting and devouring one another" (Galatians 5:15). They were fighting amongst themselves because some still believed that they needed to be circumcised (live under the law). He told them that because of Jesus, circumcision was no longer of any effect. Paul ends this chapter of Galatians with the exhortation:

"And they that are Christ's have crucified the flesh with the affections and lusts. If we live in the Spirit, let us also walk in the Spirit." (Galatians 5:24-25)

Earlier in the same chapter Paul also wrote:

"For the flesh lusteth against the Spirit, and the Spirit against the flesh: and these are contrary the one to the other: so that ye cannot do the things that ye would." (Galatians 5:17)

That means that when we are spending lots of time with the bad fruit (people and activities that do not please God), we cannot enjoy the good fruit (those things like true love, joy, peace and the like that come from the Holy Spirit). It is true that one bad apple spoils the whole bunch! Mixing the bad fruit with the good fruit will only produce bad fruit. When you spend too much time with the bad fruit you will also become tarnished.

- your attitude will change,
- you will begin to dress differently,
- even your language will change, and
- you will do things that are ungodly.

Not one of those things (the works of the flesh) mentioned in Galatians 5:19-20 can produce a good thing. They are all rotten!
My question for you today is: What are you eating, the good fruit or the bad fruit? To answer that question, consider where you spend most of your time. Do your actions line

up best with Galatians 5:19-20 or Galatians 5:22-23?

You can choose the good fruit.

WHO IS JESUS?

Key Bible Passage John 14:16 Jesus saith unto him, I am the way, the truth, and the life: no man cometh unto the Father, but by me.

Who is Jesus? He said it Himself — He is the way, the truth and the life. But what does that mean? Let's break it down:

The Way

The Way to where? Unlike many popular religions of the day, the Bible teaches that there is only One Way to Heaven — to God. And that is through Jesus. You see when God created the earth He placed the first man, Adam, in a perfect garden. And He gave him everlasting life. Everything he needed was there and Adam (and his wife Eve) actually walked and talked with God. When God placed them in that perfect place He gave them only one rule:

And the LORD God commanded the man, saying, Of every tree of the garden thou mayest freely eat: But of the tree of the knowledge of good and evil, thou shalt not eat of it: for in the day that thou eatest thereof thou shalt surely die. (Genesis 2:16-17)

The *BAD NEWS* is that Eve and her husband did eat from that tree and the relationship between God and man changed. From that moment on Adam and Eve tried to hide from God because they knew they had broken that one rule. The world that Adam and Eve had been created into was no longer perfect and their bodies began to deteriorate from life to death.

The *GOOD NEWS* is that God promised to make all things right again through a promised Messiah who would deliver mankind from the bondage of sin (Genesis 3:15). This is the theme throughout the entire Old Testament — the Promised Deliverer.

God kept His Promise and made a Way back to Him through His Son Jesus (John 1:1-14). God made Jesus sin for us, even though He was Perfect and as perfect as God in the flesh.

Jesus is the Way — the ONLY Way because we can do nothing to save ourselves from certain death. We must believe in what

Jesus did for us personally to be seen as righteous in God's eyes (2 Corinthians 5:19-21). If there was any other way, then Jesus would not have had to die. But the even *BETTER NEWS* is that Jesus proved victory over death by rising from the dead according to the Scriptures (1 Corinthians 15:1-4).

The Truth

Jesus is the Word (John 1:1-14) and the Word is Truth:

Sanctify them through thy truth: thy word is truth. (John 17:17)

The Bible says it, I believe it. It is that simple!

The Life

Jesus is how we obtain eternal or everlasting life. Without Him we will surely die:

For the wages of sin [is] death; but the gift of God [is] eternal life through Jesus Christ our Lord. (Romans 6:23)

And this is life eternal, that they might know thee the only true God, and Jesus Christ, whom thou hast sent. (John 17:3)

Verily, verily, I say unto you, He that heareth my word, and believeth on him that sent me, hath everlasting life, and shall not come into condemnation; but is passed from death unto life. (John 5:24)

For by grace are ye saved through faith; and that not of yourselves: [it is] the gift of God: Not of works, lest any man should boast. (Ephesians 2:8-9)

The Truth is that you cannot have everlasting Life in any other Way but by Jesus.

WHY DO GOOD?

Key Bible Passage: Amos 5:14-15 Seek good, and not evil, that ye may live: and so the LORD, the God of hosts, shall be with you, as ye have spoken. Hat the evil, and love the good, and establish judgment in the gate: it may be that the LORD God of hosts will be gracious unto the remnant of Joseph.

Amos is one of the twelve minor prophets that we read and hear in the Bible. He is called a minor prophet because the amount of time of his prophecy was shorter than some of the major prophets like Isiah and Daniel. Though his time was shorter, his prophecy is just as great.

In our key passage today, Amos is addressing the Jewish people when he refers to "the remnant of Joseph". Even so, throughout the Scriptures Christians are encouraged to "do good" while at the same time taught that "good works" are not what earn us a spot in Heaven (Ephesians 2:8-9; Titus 3:5-7). So then why should we do good?

That is a very good question, and I think we can let the Bible answer itself on this one. I think Jesus gave the best answer when He said: "Let your light so shine before men, that they may see your good works, and glorify your Father which is in heaven." (Matthew 5:16) So then, we should do good works so that others can see our motivation. We ought to be doing those good works so that others will ask us about God ... or at least ask us why we do them so that we have an opportunity to speak of the things of the Lord.

Other areas in Scripture teach us that our good works are the result of a loving relationship with the Lord. In this sense our good works "prove" our faith or are the "fruit" of that relationship.

For we are his workmanship, created in Christ Jesus unto good works, which God hath before ordained that we should walk in them. (Ephesians 2:10)

What doth it profit, my brethren, though a man say he hath faith, and have not works? can faith save him? If a brother or sister be naked, and destitute of daily food, And one of you say unto them, Depart in peace, be ye warmed and filled; notwithstanding ye give them not those things which are needful to the body; what doth it profit? Even so faith, if it hath not works, is dead, being alone. (James 2:14-17)

Yea, a man may say, Thou hast faith, and I have works: shew me thy faith without thy works, and I will shew thee my faith by my works. (James 2:18)

Our attitude matters too ... we should do the good works cheerfully. Others are watching, especially unbelievers. They will learn from your testimony, which is displayed in your attitude.

And whatsoever ye do in word or deed, do all in the name of the Lord Jesus, giving thanks to God and the Father by him. (Colossians 3:17)

And let us consider one another to provoke unto love and to good works: (Hebrews 10:24)

In all things shewing thyself a pattern of good works: in doctrine shewing uncorruptness, gravity, sincerity, Sound speech, that cannot be condemned; that he that is of the contrary part may be ashamed, having no evil thing to say of you. Exhort servants to be obedient unto their own masters, and to please them well in all things; not answering again; (Titus 2:7-9)

God abhors evil and for that reason we should be careful to know what is evil and avoid it. (1 Thessalonians 5:22)

Next time you do a good work, think about the motivation behind it and you will know whether or not you are doing it for the Lord. When your work is motivated out of a love for your neighbor or a love for the Lord you are doing the *right* good thing.

THE BIBLE – IN THE BEGINNING

Key Bible Passage: John 1:1 In the beginning was the Word, and the Word was with God, and the Word was God.

The Bible is a big book and one of the most popular questions I get from a new believer is, where do I start? Most people would think logically about reading a book and start at the front and then just read on through. While this might work for a mature Christian, I cannot recommend this approach for the new Christian. Why? I'm so glad you asked!

Again, the Bible is a large book, and it is made up of many smaller books — 66 to be exact. The first book, Genesis is really about "the beginning", and the last book, Revelation, is really about "the end". But the problem with starting with Genesis, for the new believer, is that it is filled with genealogies, numbers and historical accounts. When you are a new believer your main focus should be cultivating your relationship with your new-found Savior and brother, Jesus the Christ. So rather than begin at the front you might want to consider reading about the life of Jesus.

There are 5 books that focus much on the life of Jesus: Matthew, Mark, Luke, John and Acts — although Acts talks more about the "acts of the Apostles" than it does Jesus. Each of the other 4 books are called Gospels and they focus on the life of Jesus, each with their own point of view.

All of the books of the Bible were written by men whom were inspired by the Holy Spirit (2 Peter 1:21). But only two of these four Gospels were written by men that actually walked with Jesus when He was on earth. One was Matthew, a tax collector and the other was John, son of Zebedee. Both Matthew and John were of the original 12 disciples (Apostles). (Matthew 10:1-3).

It is believed that John is the one Apostle who outlived all the others, and his Gospel account was the last of the four written. He is the one mentioned in John 12:23-25 as "leaning on Jesus' bosom one of his disciples, whom Jesus loved." He was the only Apostle at the foot of the cross and Jesus trusted John with the care of His mother when He hung on the cross (John 19:25-27). John, along with James and Peter, is named by Paul in his letter to the Galatians as one of the pillars in the Church (Galatians 2:9).

John is the only one of the four Gospel writers that had a personal relationship with Jesus. He tells us that he wants us to know that Jesus is the Christ (Messiah) and the Son of God so that we "might have life through his name" (John 20:30-31). This is a book that is written with the intent to build our foundation in Jesus. It is the best book to learn about Jesus as God.

So, while the Gospel of John is not found at the front of the Bible and does not even appear as the first book of the New Testament, it does help us to know most about Jesus and the importance of our personal relationship with Him.

If you are a new believer or even one who has believed for a long time and you want to learn the most about your Savior and brother, read the Book of John — it is found as the 4th book in the New Testament.

CHOOSING THE BEST LEADER – PART 1

Key Bible Passage: Judges 21:25 In those days there was no king in Israel: every man did that which was right in his own eyes.

Many political leaders and their supporters, which do not have a Biblical world view, have adopted the position that Americans are best served when ideologies are laid aside and all parties compromise for the "greater good" of the people. While this sounds good in principle, it is this very practice that has led to the problems we have in this nation. This is because the unBiblical "greater good" ideology no longer produces ideas based on Biblically sound conservative immutable standards of right or wrong, which have benefited untold numbers of people throughout history. Instead, the unBiblical "greater good" ideology produces ideas that personally benefit the largest segment of the population at the detriment and wasteful expense of another segment of the population.

There are several points that need to be made concerning this type of thinking. First, in a representative republic, the leaders we elect are supposed to represent our values, our convictions, and our desire to do things the way we believe is best as a people. That being said, if our values, convictions, and desires are based on solid Biblical foundations of right and wrong, then any "compromise" for the "greater good" of the people is really nothing more than compromising on what is right and wrong according to God's Word.

For example, if we believe in the Biblical teaching that it is wrong to take an innocent life, then any voluntary compromise based on a "situation" is wrong. Unfortunately, most people will go out of their way to rationalize a situation, which makes it okay to compromise because of this "greater good" fallacy. This being said, the edict by the U.S. Supreme Court to legalize abortion was based on a fallacy that the privacy rights of a mother trumped the human rights of the baby. Likewise, it was argued that if abortion was readily available, then babies who were born to mothers who could not take care of them or were abusive would not have to suffer.

Unfortunately, there are two problems with both of these arguments. First, trying to justify a decision to abort a baby based on privacy rights, saying it is their body to do with what they want, ignores the fact that a baby has its own separate DNA profile from its parents, because it is a separate human being. Second, although over 50 million babies have been voluntarily slaughtered through abortion, the rates of child abuse have skyrocketed; not decreased. Nevertheless, the same tired arguments keep being made despite the overwhelming amount of evidence that shows that these arguments are nothing more than lies to convince people that what they are doing to unborn children is moral. Nothing could be farther from the truth.

When people fail to stand on Biblical principles as the standard of right and wrong and do what they think is right in their own eyes, the result is the destruction of their culture. Likewise, nations that also compromise on Biblical principles of right and wrong suffer the same destruction as well. This can be seen in the numerous collectivist countries, which existed 100 years ago, that no longer exist today. Every one of them openly rejected God's teaching and sought to implement some man-made thinking as a better way.

Unfortunately, millions of people have supported the leadership of these "enlightened thinkers," but soon found out that this way of thinking always led to suffering and death of millions before these reigns came to an end. Despite the amount of clear historical evidence and testimony of people who lived under these tyrannical systems, it has not stopped many nations today, including the United States, from seeking to implement the same in the name of "social justice."

As we see in today's verse, the Bible mentions this experience as something that the nation of Israel went through (Judges 21:25). If you read this section of Scripture in context, you find that God had told the Israelites what they should and should not do as they entered the Promised Land, however, they decided they did not want to follow His laws and counsel. This resulted in literal anarchy and bloodshed, so God raised up judges to lead them.

Like Israel, the United States has abandoned creation and enforcement of laws based on Biblical right or wrong and it has led to anarchy with ever increasing bloodshed. So, like Israel, the people do not want to be held accountable to the law, so they seek judges to decide cases in their favor with ever increasing frequency. Unfortunately, unlike Israel, more and more judges "legislate from the bench" because they too do not like the law and want to do what they think is right in their own eyes, ignoring the intent of the lawmakers. Like ancient Israel, this will lead to America's demise.

CHOOSING THE BEST LEADER – PART 2

Key Bible Passage: Proverbs 12:15 The way of a fool is right in his own eyes: but he that hearkeneth unto counsel is wise.

Continuing on from yesterday's "Things to Think on" we can see in today's verse, the Bible admonishes us not to follow the fool, but to seek the way of the wise. When the people do what is right in their own eyes and elect leaders that hold their same values, the result is representation that is foolish and devoid of wisdom. Additionally, representatives who also do what is right in their own eyes, only represent their constituents if it is beneficial to their own self. This then results in misrepresentation, which then requires elected leaders to try to please just enough people to stay in office. Too often, they do this through corruption and cronyism.

In time, the people without a Biblical worldview become disgusted with the whole process and begin to care more about what they can get out of their elected representatives than doing what is right and honorable.

Likewise, their elected representatives care only about how they can stay in office. Additionally, both then start demonizing conservatives who will not compromise their Biblically based positions as being bigoted, selfish, and hateful. Simply stated, they do this because they do not care about what is right, they only care about fulfilling their own selfish desires.

Unfortunately, instead of communicating the reason why Biblically conservative values are superior, conservatives have begun to abandon the very ideologies that have made this nation great. They have begun to compromise with those who demonize them so that they can gain more votes, money, and power. This then leads to a slippery slope where getting elected becomes a game of who can bribe the public with their own money from the treasury, because at the end of the day, the love of money is the root of all evil (1 Timothy 6:10).

The Biblically conservative ideology of right and wrong should never be compromised for popularity to win elections or for personal gain. When it is, conservatism will cease to be conservative and right and wrong will cease to underpin the ideas that have resulted and will result in God's blessings upon this nation.

When we remove God from His rightful place in the election of leaders who hold conservative principles in keeping with a Biblical worldview, we do so at our own demise.

Instead, we should seek leaders that best represent the leadership, love, and righteousness of Jesus Christ. This is because He was the perfect representative for all of humanity. When we seek Godly righteousness and goodness in our representation, we testify of the truth that lives within us, which glorifies God and enables us to prefect our love toward one another. A perfected love then can reconcile differences in ways that man cannot even imagine (Read 1 John 2:1-5).

WHO SHOULDA, WOULDA, COULDA

Key Bible Passage: 1 Corinthians 10:32-33 Give none offence, neither to the Jews, nor to the Gentiles, nor to the church of God: Even as I please all men in all things, not seeking mine own profit, but the profit of many, that they may be saved.

Sometimes people will try to set up a believer with a who shoulda, woulda, coulda, gone to hell question. They will pick out some group or demographic with the intention of getting you to say that people in that group would go to hell. While the world tries to divide humanity based on gender, skin color, ancestry, or any number of made-up labels, God only recognizes three groups of people: (1) people that were born as Jews, (2) people that were born as Gentiles, or (3) people that were born again into the church, which is the body of Christ.

You see, it does not matter who you are, what you look like, or even your gender. God does not look upon man's observation of someone's outside, God looks upon their heart (1 Samuel 16:6-7; Proverbs 26; Psalms 139).

The three groups that God uses are defined by their birth. Jews are born of the lineage of Abraham through Isaac and Gentiles are not. The church consists of former Jews and Gentiles that were born again by the Holy Spirit through faith in Christ (Galatians 3:26; John 3:1-8).

All have sinned and come short of the glory of God (Romans 3:23). This means that ALL of us - Jews, Gentiles, gay, straight, black, white, male, female, transgender, questioning, Muslim, atheist, Hindu, Buddhist - ALL of us have broken God's law and our penalty is death (Romans 6:23; 1 John 3:4). None of us in our natural state without being born again by faith in Christ are righteous before God (Galatians 3:26; Romans 3:10).

Therefore, in 1 Corinthians 10:32-33 we are called to share the gospel equally to all in a way that neither offends nor leaves out any one. HOW we present the message of the truth of salvation matters. We must present the gospel in a way that makes sure that if anyone were to stumble because of it, they stumble not because of us, but because of what they perceive as their own personal stumbling block or rock of offence, Jesus Christ. (Isaiah 8:13-15; Romans 9:30-33; 1 Peter 2:1-10; Acts 4:1-

20). May God bless us in that calling and endeavor.

WAIT ON THE LORD

Key Bible Passage: Psalms 27:14 Wait on the LORD: be of good courage, and he shall strengthen thine heart: wait, I say, on the LORD.

WOW! Sometimes it is very, very hard to wait on the LORD but it must be a very important thing to do, after all the Psalmist says "wait" more than once in this little verse. So that got me to wondering, what else does the Bible say about waiting on the Lord? What should we be doing — not doing while we wait? Let's take a look.

Rest and Don't fret

Psalms 37:7
Rest in the Lord, and wait patiently for him: fret not thyself because of him who prospereth in his way, because of the man who bringeth wicked devices to pass.

Keep His way ... be obedient to His word

Psalms 37:34

Wait on the Lord, and keep his way, and he shall exalt thee to inherit the land: when the wicked are cut off, thou shalt see it.

Don't be ashamed of why you wait and don't be confused about why you wait

Psalms 69:6
Let not them that wait on thee, O Lord God of hosts, be ashamed for my sake: let not those that seek thee be confounded for my sake, O God of Israel.

Don't forget that He is the One in Control of everything – even while you wait on Him

Psalms 123:2
Behold, as the eyes of servants look unto the hand of their masters, and as the eyes of a maiden unto the hand of her mistress; so our eyes wait upon the Lord our God, until that he have mercy upon us.

Never lose hope

Psalms 130:5
I wait for the Lord, my soul doth wait, and in his word do I hope.

Micah 7:7
Therefore I will look unto the Lord; I will wait for the God of my salvation: my God will hear me.

Remember He made a promise, and He will deliver

Proverbs 20:22
Say not thou, I will recompense evil; but wait on the Lord, and he shall save thee.

Zephaniah 3:8
Therefore wait ye upon me, saith the Lord, until the day that I rise up to the prey: for my determination is to gather the nations, that I may assemble the kingdoms, to pour upon them mine indignation, even all my fierce anger: for all the earth shall be devoured with the fire of my jealousy.

Remember it is only a matter of time, and you will be so amazed when the Lord delivers

Isaiah 40:31
But they that wait upon the Lord shall renew their strength; they shall mount up with wings

as eagles; they shall run, and not be weary; and they shall walk, and not faint.

James 5:11
Behold, we count them happy which endure. Ye have heard of the patience of Job, and have seen the end of the Lord; that the Lord is very pitiful, and of tender mercy.

Remember that God is good — all the time!

Lamentations 3:25
The Lord is good unto them that wait for him, to the soul that seeketh him.

Be quiet — be still

Lamentations 3:26
It is good that a man should both hope and quietly wait for the salvation of the Lord.

Look for the "What can I learn" rather than "Why must I wait"

Romans 5:3-5
And not only so, but we glory in tribulations also: knowing that tribulation worketh patience; And patience, experience; and experience, hope: And hope maketh not

ashamed; because the love of God is shed abroad in our hearts by the Holy Ghost which is given unto us.

Consider that in light of eternity this life circumstance is but a moment in time

Romans 8:18
For I reckon that the sufferings of this present time are not worthy to be compared with the glory which shall be revealed in us.

James 5:7-8
Be patient therefore, brethren, unto the coming of the Lord. Behold, the husbandman waiteth for the precious fruit of the earth, and hath long patience for it, until he receive the early and latter rain. Be ye also patient; stablish your hearts: for the coming of the Lord draweth nigh.

So, as we can see, God's word does not tell us to just "wait" and do nothing, but it usually tells us how to "actively wait". I pray that as you wait on the Lord you consider what His word says and don't just stop "doing".

*KJV Bible Series Ribbon certifies
KJV Bible Version Products*

You can purchase this book and other books by us at christianityeveryday.com

For a free PDF of this book let us know that you purchased this one by sending an email to us: orders@christianityeveryday.com and we will send you the file.

www.ingramcontent.com/pod-product-compliance
Lightning Source LLC
Chambersburg PA
CBHW060820050426
42449CB00008B/1744